JOURNEY

My Adirondacks

LOG BOOK

(Mt. Jo facing the high peaks in the Adirondacks)

GARRETT W. SHULTZ

MILTON & HUGO L.L.C.
4407 Park Ave., Suite 5
Union City, NJ 07087, USA

Website: *www.miltonandhugo.com*
Hotline: *1-888-778-0033*
Email: *info@miltonandhugo.com*

Ordering Information:
Quantity sales. Special discounts are granted to corporations, associations, and other organizations. For more information on these discounts, please reach out to the publisher using the contact information provided above.

Library of Congress Control Number: 2024912437
ISBN-13: 979-8-89285-192-3 [Paperback Edition]
  979-8-89285-191-6 [Digital Edition]

Rev. date: 06/24/2024

My Adirondacks Journey
Log Book

(Mt.Jo facing the high peaks in the Adirondacks)

Garrett W. Shultz

About the Author

(Garrett standing on Cascade Mountain in the Adirondacks)

Garrett is an Adirondack hiker and explorer who loves coming to the Adirondacks every year to hike and explore the beautiful geographical sites as well as the history behind them. Garrett is a college student who attends Binghamton University, pursuing a major in history. Garrett has an interest in the history behind the beautiful outdoors, so Garrett follows his dream by hiking new places every year, especially the Adirondacks, and studies the history behind the hike he completed. Garrett loves every bit of history, including World History, US History, European History, Latin American History, and the Age of Discoveries.

Garrett's first visit to the Adirondacks was in the summer of 2010, when he was 7 years old. Garrett and his family visited Lake Placid for the week. Garrett has also visited Lake George, Schroon Lake, and Lake Champlain. Garrett started his hiking journey by hiking with his mom and dad up a small trail through the woods. Garrett is an Eagle Scout with Troop 38 in Owego, NY, and has done many hiking trips and campouts throughout the Adirondacks with his Boy Scout friends. As Garrett continued his hiking journey in the Adirondacks, he faced more challenges, including rock climbing, rock scrambling, and hiking through many types of weather. By 2020, Garrett had officially recorded his first Adirondack 46er high peak, which was Rocky Peak Ridge. Since then, Garrett has been working to conquer all 46 Adirondack high peaks. Garrett also hikes for the 46Climbs fundraiser in the high peaks every year in September.

Book Information

At this point, your love for hiking in the Adirondacks has jumped to the next level. Once you start hiking in the Adirondacks, whether it's the Adirondacks 46 High Peaks, Lake Placid 9ers, or Lake George 12sters, it's always important to keep track of your hike so you can accomplish a milestone at the completion of your hikes.

This book contains the log forms to record all your hikes so you can become an Adirondack High Peaks 46er, Lake Placid 9er, Lake George 12ster, or even complete the Fire Tower Challenge. As you complete these amazing challenges, follow the details in the book on how to register yourself for the program so you can officially be recognized for your completion.

As well, when you head off to hike in the Adirondacks, be sure to pack all the right materials so your hiking trip can be enjoyable and safe. Follow the packing list in the book so you can bring the right materials for a day trip or an overnight trip. When you're hiking in the backcountry, be sure to follow the "leave no trace" principles so we can help make the environment clean and stable for many hikers and campers.

As an Adirondacks hiker and explorer, I welcome you to the "My Adirondacks Journey" log book and wish you the very best as you try to accomplish hiking the mountains in the Adirondacks.

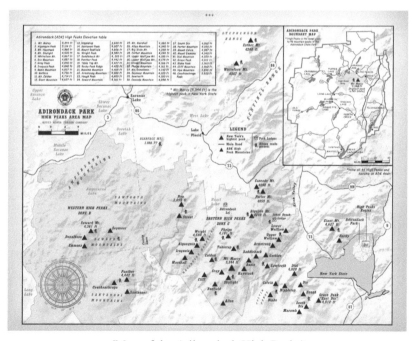

(Map of the Adirondack High Peaks)

High Peak #1: Mt. Marcy (5,344ft)

(Mt.Marcy taken from Mt.Skylight facing north)

Date of Hike:_____

Time Started:_____

Time Ended:_____

Number of People Hiking:_____

Weather Conditions:_____

Specific Details/Interesting Observations:

_____

_____

_____

_____

_____

_____

_____

_____

_____

_____

_____

_____

High Peak #2: Algonquin Peak (5,114ft)

(Algonquin peak from Adirondack lodge rd)

Date of Hike:_____

Time Started:_____

Time Ended:_____

Number of People Hiking:_____

Weather Conditions:_____

Specific Details/Interesting Observations:

_____

_____

_____

_____

_____

_____

_____

_____

_____

_____

_____

_____

_____

High Peak #3: Mt. Haystack (4,960ft)

(Mt.Haystack from Little Haystack)

Date of Hike:_____

Time Started:_____

Time Ended:_____

Number of People Hiking:_____

Weather Conditions:_____

Specific Details/Interesting Observations:

_____

_____

_____

_____

_____

_____

_____

_____

_____

_____

_____

_____

_____

_____

High Peak #4: Mt. Skylight (4,926ft)

(Mt.Skylight from the summit of Mt.Marcy)

Date of Hike:_____

Time Started:_____

Time Ended:_____

Number of People Hiking:_____

Weather Conditions:_____

Specific Details/Interesting Observations:

_____

_____

_____

_____

_____

_____

_____

_____

_____

_____

_____

_____

_____

High Peak #5: Whiteface Mt. (4,867ft)

(Whiteface Mountain)

Date of Hike:_____

Time Started:_____

Time Ended:_____

Number of People Hiking:_____

Weather Conditions:_____

Specific Details/Interesting Observations:

_____

_____

_____

_____

_____

_____

_____

_____

_____

_____

_____

_____

High Peak #6: Dix Mt. (4,857ft)

(Dix Mountain)

Date of Hike:_____

Time Started:_____

Time Ended:_____

Number of People Hiking:_____

Weather Conditions:_____

Specific Details/Interesting Observations:

_____
_____
_____
_____
_____
_____
_____
_____
_____
_____
_____
_____
_____
_____
_____
_____

High Peak #7: Gray Peak (4,840ft)

(Gray Peak from Mt.Marcy in the Winter)

Date of Hike:_____

Time Started:_____

Time Ended:_____

Number of People Hiking:_____

Weather Conditions:_____

Specific Details/Interesting Observations:

_____

_____

_____

_____

_____

_____

_____

_____

_____

_____

_____

_____

_____

High Peak #8: Iroquois Peak (4,840ft)

(Iroquois Peak from Algonquin Peak)

Date of Hike:_____

Time Started:_____

Time Ended:_____

Number of People Hiking:_____

Weather Conditions:_____

Specific Details/Interesting Observations:

_____
_____
_____
_____
_____
_____
_____
_____
_____
_____
_____
_____
_____
_____
_____

(Basin Mt. from Mt.Haystack)

Date of Hike:_____

Time Started:_____

Time Ended:_____

Number of People Hiking:_____

Weather Conditions:_____

Specific Details/Interesting Observations:

_____

_____

_____

_____

_____

_____

_____

_____

_____

_____

_____

_____

_____

High Peak #10: Gothics (4,736ft)

(Gothics from Big Slide Mountain)

Date of Hike:_____

Time Started:_____

Time Ended:_____

Number of People Hiking:_____

Weather Conditions:_____

Specific Details/Interesting Observations:

_____

_____

_____

_____

_____

_____

_____

_____

_____

_____

_____

_____

_____

High Peak #11: Mt. Colden (4,714ft)

(Mt.Colden from Wright Peak)

Date of Hike:_____

Time Started:_____

Time Ended:_____

Number of People Hiking:_____

Weather Conditions:_____

Specific Details/Interesting Observations:

_____
_____
_____
_____
_____
_____
_____
_____
_____
_____
_____
_____
_____

High Peak #12: Giant Mt. (Giant of the Valley) (4,627ft)

(Giant Mt. from Noonmark Mt.)

Date of Hike:_____

Time Started:_____

Time Ended:_____

Number of People Hiking:_____

Weather Conditions:_____

Specific Details/Interesting Observations:

_____

_____

_____

_____

_____

_____

_____

_____

_____

_____

_____

_____

_____

_____

High Peak #13: Nippletop Mt. (4,620ft)

(Nippletop Mt.)

Date of Hike:_____

Time Started:_____

Time Ended:_____

Number of People Hiking:_____

Weather Conditions:_____

Specific Details/Interesting Observations:

_____

_____

_____

_____

_____

_____

_____

_____

_____

_____

_____

_____

_____

_____

High Peak #14: Santanoni Peak (4,607ft)

(Santanoni Peak from the Ridge Between and Times Square)

Date of Hike:_____
Time Started:_____
Time Ended:_____
Number of People Hiking:_____
Weather Conditions:_____

Specific Details/Interesting Observations:

_____
_____
_____
_____
_____
_____
_____
_____
_____
_____
_____
_____
_____
_____

High Peak #15: Mt. Redfield (4,606ft)

(Mt.Redfield from Mt.Marcy)

Date of Hike:_____

Time Started:_____

Time Ended:_____

Number of People Hiking:_____

Weather Conditions:_____

Specific Details/Interesting Observations:

_____

_____

_____

_____

_____

_____

_____

_____

_____

_____

_____

_____

_____

_____

High Peak #16: Wright Peak (4,580ft)

(Wright Peak from the trail heading to Algonquin Peak)

Date of Hike:_____

Time Started:_____

Time Ended:_____

Number of People Hiking:_____

Weather Conditions:_____

Specific Details/Interesting Observations:

_____
_____
_____
_____
_____
_____
_____
_____
_____
_____
_____
_____
_____
_____
_____

High Peak #17: Saddleback Mt. (4,515ft)

(Saddleback Mountain from the southeast ascent from Basin Mountain)

Date of Hike:_____

Time Started:_____

Time Ended:_____

Number of People Hiking:_____

Weather Conditions:_____

Specific Details/Interesting Observations:

_____

_____

_____

_____

_____

_____

_____

_____

_____

_____

_____

_____

_____

High Peak #18: Panther Peak (4,442ft)

(Panther Peak from Bradley Pond leanto)

Date of Hike:_____

Time Started:_____

Time Ended:_____

Number of People Hiking:_____

Weather Conditions:_____

Specific Details/Interesting Observations:

_____

_____

_____

_____

_____

_____

_____

_____

_____

_____

_____

_____

_____

High Peak #19: Tabletop Mountain (4,427ft)

(Tabletop Mountain)

Date of Hike:_____

Time Started:_____

Time Ended:_____

Number of People Hiking:_____

Weather Conditions:_____

Specific Details/Interesting Observations:

_____

_____

_____

_____

_____

_____

_____

_____

_____

_____

_____

_____

_____

_____

High Peak #20: Rocky Peak Ridge (4,420ft)

(Rocky Peak Ridge from Giant Mountain)

Date of Hike:_____

Time Started:_____

Time Ended:_____

Number of People Hiking:_____

Weather Conditions:_____

Specific Details/Interesting Observations:

_____

_____

_____

_____

_____

_____

_____

_____

_____

_____

_____

_____

High Peak #21: Macomb Mountain (4,405ft)

(Macomb Mountain from Dix Mountain)

Date of Hike:_____

Time Started:_____

Time Ended:_____

Number of People Hiking:_____

Weather Conditions:_____

Specific Details/Interesting Observations:

_____

_____

_____

_____

_____

_____

_____

_____

_____

_____

_____

_____

_____

High Peak #22: Armstrong Mountain (4,400ft)

(Gothics (left) and Armstrong (Center) from Noonmark Mountain)

Date of Hike:_____

Time Started:_____

Time Ended:_____

Number of People Hiking:_____

Weather Conditions:_____

Specific Details/Interesting Observations:

_____

_____

_____

_____

_____

_____

_____

_____

_____

_____

_____

_____

_____

_____

_____

High Peak #23: Hough Peak (4,400ft)

(Hough Peak from the Dix Mountain Ridge Trail)

Date of Hike:_____

Time Started:_____

Time Ended:_____

Number of People Hiking:_____

Weather Conditions:_____

Specific Details/Interesting Observations:

_____

_____

_____

_____

_____

_____

_____

_____

_____

_____

_____

_____

_____

High Peak #24: Seward Mountain (4,361ft)

(Seward Mountain from Seymour Mountain)

Date of Hike:_____

Time Started:_____

Time Ended:_____

Number of People Hiking:_____

Weather Conditions:_____

Specific Details/Interesting Observations:

_____

_____

_____

_____

_____

_____

_____

_____

_____

_____

_____

_____

_____

_____

High Peak #25: Mt. Marshall (4,360ft)

(MacIntyre Range with Mt.Marshall on the far left)

Date of Hike:_____

Time Started:_____

Time Ended:_____

Number of People Hiking:_____

Weather Conditions:_____

Specific Details/Interesting Observations:

_____

_____

_____

_____

_____

_____

_____

_____

_____

_____

_____

_____

_____

_____

High Peak #26: Allen Mountain (4,340ft)

(Allen Mountain seen through the brush)

Date of Hike:_____

Time Started:_____

Time Ended:_____

Number of People Hiking:_____

Weather Conditions:_____

Specific Details/Interesting Observations:

_____

_____

_____

_____

_____

_____

_____

_____

_____

_____

_____

_____

_____

High Peak #27: Big Slide Mountain (4,240ft)

(Big Slide Mountain from Cascade Mountain)

Date of Hike:_____

Time Started:_____

Time Ended:_____

Number of People Hiking:_____

Weather Conditions:_____

Specific Details/Interesting Observations:

_____

_____

_____

_____

_____

_____

_____

_____

_____

_____

_____

_____

_____

_____

High Peak #28: Esther Mt. (4,240ft)

(Whiteface (Left) and Esther (Right) from Hurricane Mountain)

Date of Hike:_____
Time Started:_____
Time Ended:_____
Number of People Hiking:_____
Weather Conditions:_____

Specific Details/Interesting Observations:

_____
_____
_____
_____
_____
_____
_____
_____
_____
_____
_____
_____

High Peak #29: Upper Wolf Jaw (4,185ft)

(Upper Wolf Jaw from Noonmark Mountain)

Date of Hike:_____

Time Started:_____

Time Ended:_____

Number of People Hiking:_____

Weather Conditions:_____

Specific Details/Interesting Observations:

_____
_____
_____
_____
_____
_____
_____
_____
_____
_____
_____
_____
_____
_____

High Peak #30: Lower Wolf Jaw (4,175ft)

(Lower Wolf Jaw from Noonmark Mountain)

Date of Hike:_____

Time Started:_____

Time Ended:_____

Number of People Hiking:_____

Weather Conditions:_____

Specific Details/Interesting Observations:

_____

_____

_____

_____

_____

_____

_____

_____

_____

_____

_____

_____

_____

High Peak #31: Street Mountain (4,116ft)

(Street Mountain (Left) and Nye Mountain (Right))

Date of Hike:_____

Time Started:_____

Time Ended:_____

Number of People Hiking:_____

Weather Conditions:_____

Specific Details/Interesting Observations:

_____

_____

_____

_____

_____

_____

_____

_____

_____

_____

_____

_____

_____

_____

High Peak #32: Phelps Mountain (4,161ft)

(Summit of Phelps Mountain)

Date of Hike:_____

Time Started:_____

Time Ended:_____

Number of People Hiking:_____

Weather Conditions:_____

Specific Details/Interesting Observations:

_____

_____

_____

_____

_____

_____

_____

_____

_____

_____

_____

_____

_____

High Peak #33: Donaldson Mountain (4,140ft)

(Donaldson Mountain (Right) and Mt. Emmons (Left) seen from Seward Mt.)

Date of Hike:_____

Time Started:_____

Time Ended:_____

Number of People Hiking:_____

Weather Conditions:_____

Specific Details/Interesting Observations:

_____
_____
_____
_____
_____
_____
_____
_____
_____
_____
_____
_____
_____
_____
_____

High Peak #34: Seymour Mt. (4,120ft)

(Seymour Mt. (Left) seen from Donaldson Mt.)

Date of Hike:_____
Time Started:_____
Time Ended:_____
Number of People Hiking:_____
Weather Conditions:_____

Specific Details/Interesting Observations:

_____
_____
_____
_____
_____
_____
_____
_____
_____
_____
_____
_____
_____
_____

High Peak #35: Sawteeth (Sawtooth) (4,100ft)

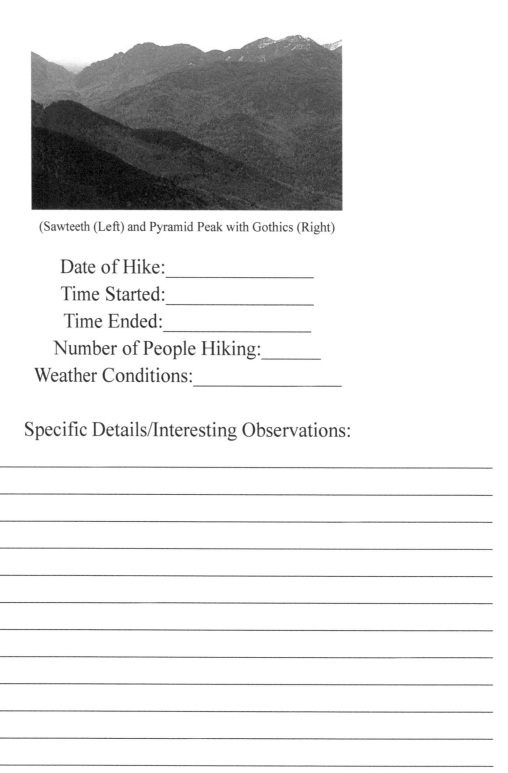

(Sawteeth (Left) and Pyramid Peak with Gothics (Right)

Date of Hike:_____

Time Started:_____

Time Ended:_____

Number of People Hiking:_____

Weather Conditions:_____

Specific Details/Interesting Observations:

_____

_____

_____

_____

_____

_____

_____

_____

_____

_____

_____

_____

_____

_____

High Peak #36: Cascade Mt. (4,098)

(Cascade Mt. from Porter Mt.)

Date of Hike:_____

Time Started:_____

Time Ended:_____

Number of People Hiking:_____

Weather Conditions:_____

Specific Details/Interesting Observations:

_____
_____
_____
_____
_____
_____
_____
_____
_____
_____
_____
_____
_____
_____
_____
_____

High Peak #37: South Dix (4,060ft)

(Summit of South Dix with Macomb and Great Range in background)

Date of Hike:_____

Time Started:_____

Time Ended:_____

Number of People Hiking:_____

Weather Conditions:_____

Specific Details/Interesting Observations:

_____

_____

_____

_____

_____

_____

_____

_____

_____

_____

_____

_____

_____

_____

_____

High Peak #38: Porter Mountain (4,059ft)

(Porter Mountain from Rooster Comb Mountain)

Date of Hike:_____

Time Started:_____

Time Ended:_____

Number of People Hiking:_____

Weather Conditions:_____

Specific Details/Interesting Observations:

_____

_____

_____

_____

_____

_____

_____

_____

_____

_____

_____

_____

_____

_____

High Peak #39: Mt. Colvin (4,057ft)

(Mt.Colvin from Lower Ausable Lake)

Date of Hike:_____

Time Started:_____

Time Ended:_____

Number of People Hiking:_____

Weather Conditions:_____

Specific Details/Interesting Observations:

_____

_____

_____

_____

_____

_____

_____

_____

_____

_____

_____

_____

_____

_____

_____

High Peak #40: Mt. Emmons (4,040ft)

(Mt.Emmons)

Date of Hike:_____

Time Started:_____

Time Ended:_____

Number of People Hiking:_____

Weather Conditions:_____

Specific Details/Interesting Observations:

_____

_____

_____

_____

_____

_____

_____

_____

_____

_____

_____

_____

_____

_____

_____

_____

High Peak #41: Dial Mt. (4,020)

(Dial Mountain (Right) with Dix Mountain and Hunters Pass (Left))

Date of Hike:_____

Time Started:_____

Time Ended:_____

Number of People Hiking:_____

Weather Conditions:_____

Specific Details/Interesting Observations:

_____

_____

_____

_____

_____

_____

_____

_____

_____

_____

_____

_____

_____

_____

_____

_____

High Peak #42: Grace Peak (4,012ft)

(Summit of Grace Peak)

Date of Hike:_____

Time Started:_____

Time Ended:_____

Number of People Hiking:_____

Weather Conditions:_____

Specific Details/Interesting Observations:

_____

_____

_____

_____

_____

_____

_____

_____

_____

_____

_____

_____

_____

_____

_____

_____

High Peak #43: Blake Peak (3,960ft)

(Blake Peak)

Date of Hike:_____

Time Started:_____

Time Ended:_____

Number of People Hiking:_____

Weather Conditions:_____

Specific Details/Interesting Observations:

_____

_____

_____

_____

_____

_____

_____

_____

_____

_____

_____

_____

_____

_____

_____

_____

High Peak #44: Cliff Mt. (3,960ft)

(Summit of Cliff Mountain)

Date of Hike:_____

Time Started:_____

Time Ended:_____

Number of People Hiking:_____

Weather Conditions:_____

Specific Details/Interesting Observations:

_____

_____

_____

_____

_____

_____

_____

_____

_____

_____

_____

_____

_____

_____

_____

High Peak #45: Nye Mt. (3,895ft)

(Street Mountain (Left) and Nye Mountain (Right)

Date of Hike:_____

Time Started:_____

Time Ended:_____

Number of People Hiking:_____

Weather Conditions:_____

Specific Details/Interesting Observations:

_____
_____
_____
_____
_____
_____
_____
_____
_____
_____
_____
_____
_____
_____
_____
_____

High Peak #46: Couchsachraga Peak (3,820ft)

(Couchsachraga Peak)

Date of Hike:_____

Time Started:_____

Time Ended:_____

Number of People Hiking:_____

Weather Conditions:_____

Specific Details/Interesting Observations:

_____

_____

_____

_____

_____

_____

_____

_____

_____

_____

_____

_____

_____

_____

CONGRATULATIONS ON FINISHING ALL 46 ADK HIGH PEAKS!!

What was your favorite high peak?

_____

What was your least favorite high peak?

_____

Date/Time Started:

_____

Date/Time Ended:

_____

What was your favorite memory?

_____

_____

_____

What was your least favorite memory?

_____

_____

_____

What lessons did you learn while hiking the ADK 46 high peaks?

_____

_____

_____

How to officially become an ADK 46er?

What is an ADK 46er? An ADK 46er refers to an individual who has climbed all 46 high peaks of the Adirondacks, completed the online registration form, received a climbing number, and submitted his or her $15 application fee! This is often referred to as the regular or 3 season round. These individuals are eligible to purchase non-winter emblem items in our online store.

What is an ADK Winter 46er? An ADK Winter 46er refers to an individual who has climbed all 46 high peaks of the Adirondacks during the winter season **(December 21 to March 21 inclusive),** completed the online registration form, and submitted his or her $15 Winter application fee. An individual may become an ADK 46er having only completed a Winter round. A "W" will be added after your climbing number to signify this accomplishment. These individuals are eligible to purchase winter emblem items in our online store.

1. Hike all 46 ADK High Peaks- Fill out the log book as you go.

2. Complete ALL required sections of the **OFFICIAL finisher form** available on the website and pay your $15 initial application fee for each new member.

3. Once you submit your finisher form and pay your dues, you should receive an "Official Letter of Congratulations" in a confirmation email with your assigned 46er climbing number. Once your letter is received, you will become eligible to purchase merchandise and emblem items in our online store.

Lake Placid 9er #1: Hurricane Mountain (3,678ft)

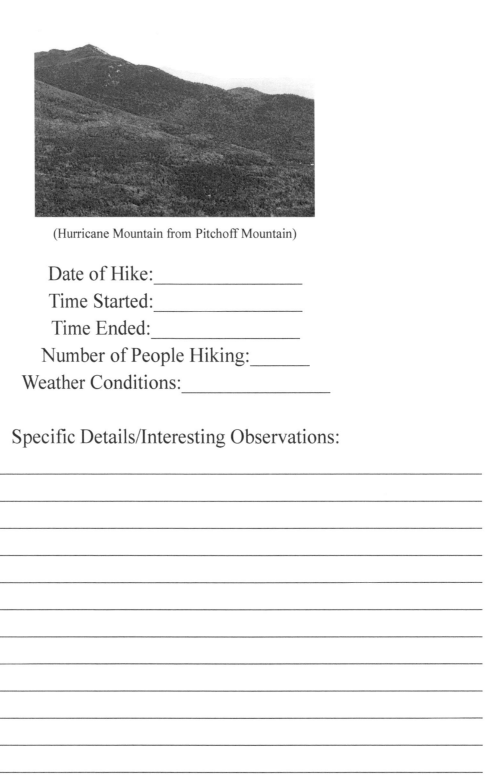

(Hurricane Mountain from Pitchoff Mountain)

Date of Hike:_____

Time Started:_____

Time Ended:_____

Number of People Hiking:_____

Weather Conditions:_____

Specific Details/Interesting Observations:

_____

_____

_____

_____

_____

_____

_____

_____

_____

_____

_____

_____

_____

_____

Lake Placid 9er #2: Pitchoff Mountain (3,500ft)

(Pitchoff Mountain from NY 73)

Date of Hike:_____

Time Started:_____

Time Ended:_____

Number of People Hiking:_____

Weather Conditions:_____

Specific Details/Interesting Observations:

_____
_____
_____
_____
_____
_____
_____
_____
_____
_____
_____
_____
_____
_____

Lake Placid 9er #3: Catamount Mountain (3,169ft)

(Catamount Mountain below the summit)

Date of Hike:_____

Time Started:_____

Time Ended:_____

Number of People Hiking:_____

Weather Conditions:_____

Specific Details/Interesting Observations:

_____

_____

_____

_____

_____

_____

_____

_____

_____

_____

_____

_____

_____

_____

Lake Placid 9er #4: Mt. Van Hoevenberg (2,940ft)

(Mt.Van Hoevenberg summit with Mt.Colden and MacIntyre Range in the background)

Date of Hike:_____

Time Started:_____

Time Ended:_____

Number of People Hiking:_____

Weather Conditions:_____

Specific Details/Interesting Observations:

_____

_____

_____

_____

_____

_____

_____

_____

_____

_____

_____

_____

_____

_____

Lake Placid 9er #5: Mt. Jo (2,876ft)

(Summit of Mt.Jo with Heart Lake, MacIntyre Range, Mt.Colden, and Mt.Marcy in the distance)

Date of Hike:_____

Time Started:_____

Time Ended:_____

Number of People Hiking:_____

Weather Conditions:_____

Specific Details/Interesting Observations:

_____

_____

_____

_____

_____

_____

_____

_____

_____

_____

_____

_____

_____

_____

Lake Placid 9er #6: Big Crow Mt. (2,815ft)

(Summit of Big Crow Mountain)

Date of Hike:_____

Time Started:_____

Time Ended:_____

Number of People Hiking:_____

Weather Conditions:_____

Specific Details/Interesting Observations:

_____

_____

_____

_____

_____

_____

_____

_____

_____

_____

_____

_____

_____

_____

Lake Placid 9er #7: Bear Den Mt. (2,650ft)

(Bear Den Mountain)

Date of Hike:_____

Time Started:_____

Time Ended:_____

Number of People Hiking:_____

Weather Conditions:_____

Specific Details/Interesting Observations:

_____

_____

_____

_____

_____

_____

_____

_____

_____

_____

_____

_____

_____

_____

_____

Lake Placid 9er #8: Baxter Mt. (2,440ft)

(Summit of Baxter Mountain)

Date of Hike:_____

Time Started:_____

Time Ended:_____

Number of People Hiking:_____

Weather Conditions:_____

Specific Details/Interesting Observations:

_____

_____

_____

_____

_____

_____

_____

_____

_____

_____

_____

_____

_____

_____

Lake Placid 9er #9: Cobble Hill (2,332ft)

(View of Cobble Hill)

Date of Hike:_____

Time Started:_____

Time Ended:_____

Number of People Hiking:_____

Weather Conditions:_____

Specific Details/Interesting Observations:

_____

_____

_____

_____

_____

_____

_____

_____

_____

_____

_____

_____

_____

_____

CONGRATULATIONS ON FINISHING THE LAKE PLACID 9ERS!!

What was your favorite mountain?

_____

What was your least favorite mountain?

_____

Date/Time Started:

_____

Date/Time Ended:

_____

What was your favorite memory?

_____

_____

_____

What was your least favorite memory?

_____

_____

_____

What lessons did you learn while hiking the Lake Placid 9ers?

_____

_____

_____

How to officially become a Lake Placid 9er?

1. Hike all the Lake Placid 9er- Fill out the log book as you go.

2. Upon successful completion of all the LP 9 peaks, please submit the registration form to:

    Lake Placid 9er
    PO Box 1310
    Lake Placid, NY 12946

3. Be sure to enclose your $12 registration fee. Checks can be made payable to 'Lake Placid 9er.'

4. We'll ship you your official LP 9er finisher's patch, sticker, and official finisher's card.

Please allow 3-4 weeks for processing!!

Lake George 12ster #1: Black Mt. (2,665ft)

(Black Mountain from Lake George)

Date of Hike:_____

Time Started:_____

Time Ended:_____

Number of People Hiking:_____

Weather Conditions:_____

Specific Details/Interesting Observations:

_____

_____

_____

_____

_____

_____

_____

_____

_____

_____

_____

_____

_____

_____

Lake George 12ster #2: Erebus Mt. (2,527ft)

(Erebus Mountain)

Date of Hike:_____

Time Started:_____

Time Ended:_____

Number of People Hiking:_____

Weather Conditions:_____

Specific Details/Interesting Observations:

_____

_____

_____

_____

_____

_____

_____

_____

_____

_____

_____

_____

_____

_____

_____

Lake George 12ster #3: Sleeping Beauty (2,347ft)

(Summit of Sleeping Beauty)

Date of Hike:_____

Time Started:_____

Time Ended:_____

Number of People Hiking:_____

Weather Conditions:_____

Specific Details/Interesting Observations:

_____
_____
_____
_____
_____
_____
_____
_____
_____
_____
_____
_____
_____
_____

Lake George 12ster #4: Buck Mt. (2,334ft)

(Summit of Buck Mountain facing Lake George)

Date of Hike:_____

Time Started:_____

Time Ended:_____

Number of People Hiking:_____

Weather Conditions:_____

Specific Details/Interesting Observations:

_____

_____

_____

_____

_____

_____

_____

_____

_____

_____

_____

_____

_____

Lake George 12ster #5: Five Mile Mt. (2,256ft)

(Summit view of Five Mile Mountain)

Date of Hike:_____

Time Started:_____

Time Ended:_____

Number of People Hiking:_____

Weather Conditions:_____

Specific Details/Interesting Observations:

_____

_____

_____

_____

_____

_____

_____

_____

_____

_____

_____

_____

_____

Lake George 12ster #6: Huckleberry Mt. (2,232ft)

(Huckleberry Mountain from Murphy Lake)

Date of Hike:_____

Time Started:_____

Time Ended:_____

Number of People Hiking:_____

Weather Conditions:_____

Specific Details/Interesting Observations:

_____

_____

_____

_____

_____

_____

_____

_____

_____

_____

_____

_____

_____

Lake George 12ster #7: Thomas Mt. (2,031ft)

(Thomas Mountain Summit)

Date of Hike:_____

Time Started:_____

Time Ended:_____

Number of People Hiking:_____

Weather Conditions:_____

Specific Details/Interesting Observations:

_____

_____

_____

_____

_____

_____

_____

_____

_____

_____

_____

_____

_____

_____

Lake George 12ster #8: Brown Mt. (1,966ft)

(View of Brown Mountain)

Date of Hike:_____

Time Started:_____

Time Ended:_____

Number of People Hiking:_____

Weather Conditions:_____

Specific Details/Interesting Observations:

_____

_____

_____

_____

_____

_____

_____

_____

_____

_____

_____

_____

_____

Lake George 12ster #9: Cat Mt. (1,956ft)

(Cat Mountain with Lake George in the background)

Date of Hike:_____

Time Started:_____

Time Ended:_____

Number of People Hiking:_____

Weather Conditions:_____

Specific Details/Interesting Observations:

_____

_____

_____

_____

_____

_____

_____

_____

_____

_____

_____

_____

_____

_____

Lake George 12ster #10: Fifth Peak (1,813ft)

(Lake George from the summit of Fifth Peak)

Date of Hike:_____

Time Started:_____

Time Ended:_____

Number of People Hiking:_____

Weather Conditions:_____

Specific Details/Interesting Observations:

_____

_____

_____

_____

_____

_____

_____

_____

_____

_____

_____

_____

_____

_____

Lake George 12ster #11: French Point Mt. (1,756ft)

(The summit of French Point Mountain)

Date of Hike:_____

Time Started:_____

Time Ended:_____

Number of People Hiking:_____

Weather Conditions:_____

Specific Details/Interesting Observations:

_____

_____

_____

_____

_____

_____

_____

_____

_____

_____

_____

_____

_____

Lake George 12ster #12: First Peak (1,586ft)

(View of First Peak)

Date of Hike:_____

Time Started:_____

Time Ended:_____

Number of People Hiking:_____

Weather Conditions:_____

Specific Details/Interesting Observations:

_____

_____

_____

_____

_____

_____

_____

_____

_____

_____

_____

_____

_____

CONGRATULATIONS ON FINISHING THE LAKE GEORGE 12STERS!!

What was your favorite mountain?

_____

What was your least favorite mountain?

_____

Date/Time Started:

_____

Date/Time Ended:

_____

What was your favorite memory?

_____

_____

_____

What was your least favorite memory?

_____

_____

_____

What lessons did you learn while hiking the Lake George 12sters?

_____

_____

_____

How to officially become a Lake George 12ster?

What is a Lake George 12ster? Similar to the well-known Adirondack 46er, the Lake George 12ster challenges hikers to summit a certain number of peaks. Hikers who complete this challenge and register to be a Lake George 12ster are officially recognized for their achievement with a patch.

There are 12 peaks to climb as part of the Lake George 12ster. In total, this amounts to 40 miles and 9,000 feet of elevation gain. You can hike the peaks in any order, but some variations of the challenge include time restrictions.

1. Hike all 12 Lake George Mountains- Fill out the log book as you go.

2. Complete the Registration Form and email it to hello@lakegeorge12ster.com

3. Registration includes certificate, 12ster number, sticker, and patch.

Processing might take 3-4 weeks!!

Fire Tower #1: Mt. Adams (3,250ft)

(View from Mt.Adams Fire Tower)

Date of Hike:_____

Time Started:_____

Time Ended:_____

Number of People Hiking:_____

Weather Conditions:_____

Specific Details/Interesting Observations:

_____

_____

_____

_____

_____

_____

_____

_____

_____

_____

_____

_____

_____

_____

Fire Tower #2: Mt. Arab (2,546ft)

(View from Mt.Arab)

Date of Hike:_____

Time Started:_____

Time Ended:_____

Number of People Hiking:_____

Weather Conditions:_____

Specific Details/Interesting Observations:

_____
_____
_____
_____
_____
_____
_____
_____
_____
_____
_____
_____
_____
_____

Fire Tower #3: Azure Mt. (2,518ft)

(View from Azure Mt.)

Date of Hike:_____

Time Started:_____

Time Ended:_____

Number of People Hiking:_____

Weather Conditions:_____

Specific Details/Interesting Observations:

_____

_____

_____

_____

_____

_____

_____

_____

_____

_____

_____

_____

_____

_____

_____

_____

Fire Tower #4: Bald Mt. (2,350ft)

(Summit of Bald Mountain)

Date of Hike:_____

Time Started:_____

Time Ended:_____

Number of People Hiking:_____

Weather Conditions:_____

Specific Details/Interesting Observations:

_____

_____

_____

_____

_____

_____

_____

_____

_____

_____

_____

_____

_____

Fire Tower #5: Belfry Mt. (1,850ft)

(View from Belfry Mountain)

Date of Hike:_____

Time Started:_____

Time Ended:_____

Number of People Hiking:_____

Weather Conditions:_____

Specific Details/Interesting Observations:

_____

_____

_____

_____

_____

_____

_____

_____

_____

_____

_____

_____

_____

_____

Fire Tower #6: Black Mt. (2,641ft)

(Summit of Black Mountain)

Date of Hike:_____

Time Started:_____

Time Ended:_____

Number of People Hiking:_____

Weather Conditions:_____

Specific Details/Interesting Observations:

_____
_____
_____
_____
_____
_____
_____
_____
_____
_____
_____
_____
_____
_____
_____
_____
_____

Fire Tower #7: Blue Mt. (3,750ft)

(View from Blue Mountain)

Date of Hike:_____

Time Started:_____

Time Ended:_____

Number of People Hiking:_____

Weather Conditions:_____

Specific Details/Interesting Observations:

_____

_____

_____

_____

_____

_____

_____

_____

_____

_____

_____

_____

_____

Fire Tower #8: Buck Mt. (2,631ft)

(View from Buck Mountain)

Date of Hike:_____

Time Started:_____

Time Ended:_____

Number of People Hiking:_____

Weather Conditions:_____

Specific Details/Interesting Observations:

_____

_____

_____

_____

_____

_____

_____

_____

_____

_____

_____

_____

_____

_____

Fire Tower #9: Cathedral Rock (1,680ft)

(Cathedral Fire Tower in the Winter)

Date of Hike:_____
Time Started:_____
Time Ended:_____
Number of People Hiking:_____
Weather Conditions:_____

Specific Details/Interesting Observations:

_____
_____
_____
_____
_____
_____
_____
_____
_____
_____
_____
_____
_____

Fire Tower #10: Goodnow Mt. (2,690ft)

(View of Goodnow Mountain)

Date of Hike:_____

Time Started:_____

Time Ended:_____

Number of People Hiking:_____

Weather Conditions:_____

Specific Details/Interesting Observations:

_____

_____

_____

_____

_____

_____

_____

_____

_____

_____

_____

_____

_____

_____

_____

_____

_____

Fire Tower #11: Gore Mt. (3,563ft)

(View from Gore Mountain)

Date of Hike:_____

Time Started:_____

Time Ended:_____

Number of People Hiking:_____

Weather Conditions:_____

Specific Details/Interesting Observations:

_____

_____

_____

_____

_____

_____

_____

_____

_____

_____

_____

_____

_____

_____

_____

Fire Tower #12: Hadley Mt. (2,654ft)

(View from Hadley Mountain)

Date of Hike:_____

Time Started:_____

Time Ended:_____

Number of People Hiking:_____

Weather Conditions:_____

Specific Details/Interesting Observations:

_____

_____

_____

_____

_____

_____

_____

_____

_____

_____

_____

_____

_____

_____

_____

Fire Tower #13: Hurricane Mt. (3,678ft)

(Summit of Hurricane Mountain)

Date of Hike:_____

Time Started:_____

Time Ended:_____

Number of People Hiking:_____

Weather Conditions:_____

Specific Details/Interesting Observations:

_____

_____

_____

_____

_____

_____

_____

_____

_____

_____

_____

_____

_____

_____

_____

_____

Fire Tower #14: Kane Mt. (2,180ft)

(View from Kane Mountain)

Date of Hike:_____

Time Started:_____

Time Ended:_____

Number of People Hiking:_____

Weather Conditions:_____

Specific Details/Interesting Observations:

_____

_____

_____

_____

_____

_____

_____

_____

_____

_____

_____

_____

_____

_____

_____

Fire Tower #15: Loon Lake Mt. (3,311ft)

(View from Loon Lake Mountain)

Date of Hike:_____

Time Started:_____

Time Ended:_____

Number of People Hiking:_____

Weather Conditions:_____

Specific Details/Interesting Observations:

_____

_____

_____

_____

_____

_____

_____

_____

_____

_____

_____

_____

_____

_____

_____

Fire Tower #16: Lyon Mt. (3,819ft)

(View from Lyon Mountain)

Date of Hike:_____

Time Started:_____

Time Ended:_____

Number of People Hiking:_____

Weather Conditions:_____

Specific Details/Interesting Observations:

_____

_____

_____

_____

_____

_____

_____

_____

_____

_____

_____

_____

_____

_____

_____

Fire Tower #17: Owls Head Mt. (2,812ft)

(View from Owls Head Mountain)

Date of Hike:_____

Time Started:_____

Time Ended:_____

Number of People Hiking:_____

Weather Conditions:_____

Specific Details/Interesting Observations:

_____

_____

_____

_____

_____

_____

_____

_____

_____

_____

_____

_____

_____

_____

_____

Fire Tower #18: Pillsbury Mt. (3,597ft)

(View from Pillsbury Mountain)

Date of Hike:_____

Time Started:_____

Time Ended:_____

Number of People Hiking:_____

Weather Conditions:_____

Specific Details/Interesting Observations:

_____

_____

_____

_____

_____

_____

_____

_____

_____

_____

_____

_____

_____

_____

_____

Fire Tower #19: Poke-O-Moonshine Mt. (2,180ft)

(Summit of Poke-O-Moonshine Mountain)

Date of Hike:_____

Time Started:_____

Time Ended:_____

Number of People Hiking:_____

Weather Conditions:_____

Specific Details/Interesting Observations:

_____

_____

_____

_____

_____

_____

_____

_____

_____

_____

_____

_____

_____

Fire Tower #20: Snowy Mt. (3,898ft)

(View from Snowy Mountain)

Date of Hike:_____

Time Started:_____

Time Ended:_____

Number of People Hiking:_____

Weather Conditions:_____

Specific Details/Interesting Observations:

_____

_____

_____

_____

_____

_____

_____

_____

_____

_____

_____

_____

_____

_____

Fire Tower #21: Spruce Mt. (2,009ft)

(Summit of Spruce Mountain)

Date of Hike:_____

Time Started:_____

Time Ended:_____

Number of People Hiking:_____

Weather Conditions:_____

Specific Details/Interesting Observations:

_____

_____

_____

_____

_____

_____

_____

_____

_____

_____

_____

_____

_____

_____

_____

Fire Tower #22: Stillwater Mt. (2,244ft)

(View from Stillwater Mountain)

Date of Hike:_____

Time Started:_____

Time Ended:_____

Number of People Hiking:_____

Weather Conditions:_____

Specific Details/Interesting Observations:

_____

_____

_____

_____

_____

_____

_____

_____

_____

_____

_____

_____

_____

_____

_____

_____

Fire Tower #23: St. Regis Mt. (2,874ft)

(Summit of St. Regis Mountain)

Date of Hike:_____

Time Started:_____

Time Ended:_____

Number of People Hiking:_____

Weather Conditions:_____

Specific Details/Interesting Observations:

_____

_____

_____

_____

_____

_____

_____

_____

_____

_____

_____

_____

_____

_____

Fire Tower #24: Swede Mt. (1,900ft)

(View from Swede Mountain)

Date of Hike:_____

Time Started:_____

Time Ended:_____

Number of People Hiking:_____

Weather Conditions:_____

Specific Details/Interesting Observations:

_____

_____

_____

_____

_____

_____

_____

_____

_____

_____

_____

_____

_____

Fire Tower #25: Vanderwhacker Mt. (3,389ft)

(View from Vanderwhacker Mountain)

Date of Hike:_____

Time Started:_____

Time Ended:_____

Number of People Hiking:_____

Weather Conditions:_____

Specific Details/Interesting Observations:

_____

_____

_____

_____

_____

_____

_____

_____

_____

_____

_____

_____

_____

Fire Tower #26: Wakely Mt. (3,744ft)

(View from Wakely Mountain)

Date of Hike:_____

Time Started:_____

Time Ended:_____

Number of People Hiking:_____

Weather Conditions:_____

Specific Details/Interesting Observations:

_____

_____

_____

_____

_____

_____

_____

_____

_____

_____

_____

_____

_____

_____

_____

Fire Tower #27: Woodhull Mt. (2,365ft)

(Summit of Woodhull Mountain)

Date of Hike:_____

Time Started:_____

Time Ended:_____

Number of People Hiking:_____

Weather Conditions:_____

Specific Details/Interesting Observations:

_____

_____

_____

_____

_____

_____

_____

_____

_____

_____

_____

_____

_____

_____

_____

CONGRATULATIONS ON FINISHING THE FIRE TOWER CHALLENGE!!

What was your favorite fire tower?

_____

What was your least favorite fire towel?

_____

Date/Time Started:

_____

Date/Time Ended:

_____

What was your favorite memory?

_____

_____

_____

What was your least favorite memory?

_____

_____

_____

What lessons did you learn while hiking the different fire towers?

_____

_____

_____

How to officially become a member of the Fire Tower Challenge?

Must summit 18 of the 27 Adirondack fire tower peaks and all 5 of the Catskills fire tower peaks, for a total of 23 fire tower mountains. Each mountain listed below should have a standing fire tower on the date of your ascent.

Catskill Fire Towers:

- Balsam Lake (3,730ft)
- Hunter Mt. (4,039ft)
- Overlook Mt. (3,140ft)
- Red Hill (2,914ft)
- Tremper Mt. (2,724ft)

The Adirondack Mountain Club, which started this challenge in 2001, asks that in addition to recording the dates of your climbs that you take note of additional details like the weather and wildlife sightings.

LEAVE NO TRACE PRINCIPLES:

Plan Ahead and Prepare

- Know the regulations and special concerns for the area you'll visit.
- Prepare for extreme weather, hazards, and emergencies.
- Schedule your trip to avoid times of high use.
- Visit in small groups when possible. Consider splitting larger groups into smaller groups.
- Repackage food to minimize waste.
- Use a map and compass or GPS to eliminate the use of marking paint, rock cairns or flagging.

Travel and Camp on Durable Surfaces

- Durable surfaces include maintained trails and designated campsites, rock, gravel, sand, dry grasses or snow.
- Protect riparian areas by camping at least 200 feet from lakes and streams
- Good campsites are found, not made. Altering a site is not necessary.

Dispose of Waste Properly

- Pack it in, pack it out. Inspect your campsite, food preparation areas, and rest areas for trash or spilled foods. Pack out all trash, leftover food and litter.
- Utilize toilet facilities whenever possible. Otherwise, deposit solid human waste in catholes dug 6 to 8 inches deep, at least 200 feet from water, camp and trails. Cover and disguise the cathole when finished.
- Pack out toilet paper and hygiene products.
- To wash yourself or your dishes, carry water 200 feet away from streams or lakes and use small amounts of biodegradable soap. Scatter strained dishwater.

Leave What You Find

- Preserve the past: examine, photograph, but do not touch cultural or historic structures and artifacts.
- Leave rocks, plants and other natural objects as you find them.
- Avoid introducing or transporting non-native species.
- Do not build structures, furniture, or dig trenches.

Minimize Campfire Impacts

- Campfires can cause lasting impacts to the environment. Use a lightweight stove for cooking and enjoy a candle lantern for light.
- Where fires are permitted, use established fire rings, fire pans, or mound fires.
- Keep fires small. Only use down and dead wood from the ground that can be broken by hand.
- Burn all wood and coals to ash, put out campfires completely, then scatter cool ashes.

Respect Wildlife

- Observe wildlife from a distance. Do not follow or approach them.
- Never feed animals. Feeding wildlife damages their health, alters natural behaviors, [habituates them to humans], and exposes them to predators and other dangers.
- Protect wildlife and your food by storing rations and trash securely.
- Control pets at all times, or leave them at home.
- Avoid wildlife during sensitive times: mating, nesting, raising young, or winter.

Be Considerate of Other Visitors

- Respect other visitors and protect the quality of their experience.
- Be courteous. Yield to other users on the trail.
- Step to the downhill side of the trail when encountering pack stock.
- Take breaks and camp away from trails and other visitors.
- Let nature's sounds prevail. Avoid loud voices and noises.

The Ultimate Camping Checklist:

Many campgrounds have drinkable water. If not, bring your own, or be prepared to treat water if there's a water source. And depending on how remote your campsite is, navigation tools such as a map, compass and/or GPS may be required

CAMPSITE

- [ ] Tent *(with footprint & stakes)*
- [ ] Sleeping bags
- [ ] Sleeping pads
- [ ] Camping pillow
- [ ] Headlamps or flashlights *(with extra batteries)*
- [ ] Camp chairs
- [ ] Camp table *(if no picnic table at campsite)*
- [ ] Lantern *(with mantles and fuel/batteries if needed)*

Optional:

- [ ] Hammock

- [ ] Sunshade, tarp, or screen house
- [ ] Cots
- [ ] Sleeping bag liners
- [ ] Firewood *(sourced near campsite)*
- [ ] Camp rug
- [ ] Tablecloth and clips *(or tape)*
- [ ] Clothesline *(with clips)*
- [ ] _____
- [ ] _____
- [ ] _____
- [ ] _____

CAMPSITE EXTRAS

- [ ] Solar and portable power
- [ ] Binoculars
- [ ] Navigation tools
- [ ] Field guides *(flowers, insects)*
- [ ] Star chart/night-sky identifier
- [ ] Book/reading material
- [ ] Notebook and pen/pencil
- [ ] Music player *(with headphones)*
- [ ] Games and toys
- [ ] Dog gear
- [ ] Dry bags, stuff sacks or clear plastic bins to store items
- [ ] _____

KITCHEN

- [ ] Stove and fuel
- [ ] Matches/ lighter/ firestarter
- [ ] Cook pots *(with pot holder)*
- [ ] Frying pan
- [ ] Eating utensils
- [ ] Cooking utensils
- [ ] Bottle opener, can opener, and corkscrew
- [ ] Sharp knife
- [ ] Plates/bowls
- [ ] Mugs/cups
- [ ] Cutting board
- [ ] Cooler

- [ ] Ice or ice substitutes
- [ ] Water bottles
- [ ] Camp sink *(or wash bins)*
- [ ] Biodegradable soap
- [ ] Pot scrubber/sponge(s)
- [ ] Trash and recycling bags
- [ ] Dish towel

Optional:

- [ ] Camp grill and fuel
- [ ] Grill rack
- [ ] Griddle
- [ ] Dutch oven

- [ ] Charcoal
- [ ] Portable coffee/tea maker
- [ ] Rolling ice cream maker
- [ ] Marshmallow/hot dog roasting forks
- [ ] Small food-storage conainers, bags and foil
- [ ] Large water jugs
- [ ] Large, clear plastic bins *(for storing kitchen gear)*
- [ ] _____
- [ ] _____
- [ ] _____

🎒 CLOTHING/FOOTWEAR

- ☐ Moisture-wicking underwear
- ☐ Moisture-wicking T-shirts
- ☐ Quick-drying pants/shorts
- ☐ Long-sleeve shirts (*for sun and bugs*)
- ☐ Lightweight fleece or jacket
- ☐ Boots or shoes suited to terrain
- ☐ Socks (*synthetic or wool*)
- ☐ Sleepwear
- ☐ Sunglasses (*with retainer leash*)
- ☐ Sun hat

Additional items for rainy and/or cold weather:

- ☐ Rainwear (*jacket and pants*)
- ☐ Long underwear
- ☐ Warm insulated jacket or vest
- ☐ Fleece pants
- ☐ Gloves or mittens
- ☐ Warm hat

Optional:

- ☐ Swimsuits
- ☐ Water sandals
- ☐ In-camp sandals or booties
- ☐ Bandanas or Buffs
- ☐ _____
- ☐ _____

🧴 HEALTH & HYGIENE

- ☐ Toilet paper
- ☐ Hand sanitizer
- ☐ Toothbrush and toothpaste
- ☐ Toiletry kit
- ☐ Quick-dry towel
- ☐ Menstrual and urinary products
- ☐ Prescription medications
- ☐ First-aid kit or supplies

Sun and bug protection:

- ☐ Sunscreen
- ☐ Lip balm
- ☐ Insect repellent
- ☐ Insect repellent candles

Optional:

- ☐ Sanitation trowel (*if no toilets*)
- ☐ Baby wipes
- ☐ Alcohol or antiseptic wipes
- ☐ Mirror
- ☐ Brush/comb
- ☐ Cosmetics
- ☐ Spare eyeglasses/contact lens supplies
- ☐ Eyeshades
- ☐ Earplugs
- ☐ Portable camp shower
- ☐ _____
- ☐ _____

🔧 TOOLS & REPAIRS

- ☐ Multi-tool
- ☐ Duct tape
- ☐ Extra cord
- ☐ Tent-pole repair sleeve
- ☐ Pad/Mattress repair kit
- ☐ Mallet or hammer (*for hammering tent stakes*)
- ☐ Saw or axe (*for cutting firewood*)
- ☐ Small broom and dustpan
- ☐ _____
- ☐ _____

💳 PERSONAL ITEMS

- ☐ Credit card and/or cash
- ☐ ID
- ☐ Cell phone
- ☐ Campsite reservation confirmation (*if required*)
- ☐ _____
- ☐ _____

Adirondack History Facts:

- The first users of this landscape were two Native American tribes, the Mohawks and the Algonquins.

- Adirondack mountains due to their harsh climate and rugged landscape. Nevertheless, the tribes did use the lands for hunting and fishing, and as a thoroughfare to other areas of the state. In fact, it has been said that the word "Adirondack" means "Barkeater" or "those who eat trees" in the language of the Mohawks.

- Geologist Ebenezer Emmons officially named the region the "Adirondacks" in 1838.

- The Adirondacks were also a major backdrop for the French and Indian War and later Revolutionary War. In fact, there are historical landmarks along the shores of Lake Champlain that still stand today.

- The first European to visit the Adirondacks was Samuel De Champlain, and he discovered what is now Lake Champlain and the eastern border of the Adirondack Park. Slowly, colonization of the area began.

- In 1894 the State of New York protected the Adirondack Park as "Forever Wild" under Article XIV of the New York State Constitution. This means that the public land is constitutionally protected from being sold or leased by the state.

- After World War II, the construction of state highway I-87 or the "Adirondack Northway," changed the face of tourism in the Adirondacks. Tourists' taste for hotel and motel accommodations over guest houses took precedence.

- The winter Olympics drew crowds when they were held in Lake Placid in 1932 and 1980. Now, the preference for a more personal stay has brought back bed and breakfasts, and more local home rental accommodations to fit the needs of those coming up to the Adirondacks for a visit.

Photo Credit:

- Mt. Marcy- Rocfan275
- Algonquin Peak- Jean-Nicholas Lajoie- May 21st, 2007
- Mt. Haystack. Daniel Tripp
- Mt. Skylight- M.L. Devall- July 17th, 2007
- Whiteface Mountain- Mwanner- November, 12th, 2008
- Dix Mountain- Theedster123- October 6th, 2007
- Gray Peak- Aepstein607- May 24th, 2007
- Iroquois Peak- Aepstein607- May 24th, 2007
- Basin Mountain- Aepstein607- July 18th, 2007
- Gothics- Mwanner- June 11th, 2008
- Mt. Colden- Mwanner- September 18th, 2008
- Giant Mountain- Newark777- February 9th, 2007
- Nippletop Mountain- Adirondack.net
- Santanoni Peak- Petersent- April 6th, 1996
- Mt. Redfield- Adirondack.net
- Wright Peak- Timothy Hutchings- August 10th, 2014
- Saddleback Mountain- PhacopsRana- August 16th, 2005
- Panther Peak- Petersent- April 6th, 1996
- Tabletop Mountain- Adirondack.net
- Rocky Peak Ridge- Theedster123- August 11th, 2007
- Macomb Mountain- Adirondack.net
- Armstrong Mountain- Mwanner- May 7th, 2008
- Hough Peak- Petersent- August 2nd, 1998
- Seward Mountain- Petersent- March 26, 1995
- Mt. Marshall- Holmes
- Allen Mountain- Adirondack.net
- Big Slide Mountain- Mwanner- May 3rd, 2008
- Esther Mountain- Mwanner- May 5th, 2008
- Upper Wolf Jaw- Mwanner- May 7th, 2008
- Lower Wolf Jaw- Mwanner- May 7th, 2008
- Street Mountain- lakeplacid.com
- Phelps Mountain- lakeplacid.com
- Donaldson Mountain- Petersent- September 1st, 1996
- Seymour Mountain- Petersent- March 31st, 1995
- Sawteeth- Mwanner- May 5th, 2008
- Cascade Mountain- Laurent Gélinas- April 21st, 2013
- South Dix- Adirondack.net
- Porter Mountain- Mwanner- June 12th, 2008

- Mt. Colvin- Petersent- April 15th, 1995
- Mt. Emmons- Adirondack.net
- Dial Mountain- Mwanner- May 7th, 2008
- Grace Peak- Adirondack.net
- Blake Peak- lakeplacid.com
- Cliff Mountain- lakeplacid.com
- Nye Mountain- lakeplacid.com
- Couchsachraga Peak- Holmes
- Hurricane Mountain- Mwanner- May 28th, 2008
- Pitchoff Mountain- Mwanner- May 2nd, 2008
- Catamount Mountain- Protectadks.com- August 29th, 2020
- Mt. Van Hoevenberg- Lakeplaicdclublodges.com- August 26th, 2020
- Mt. Jo- Pureadirondacks.com
- Big Crow Mountain- Protectadks.com- March 28th, 2021
- Bear Den Mountain- Pureadirondacks.com
- Baxter Mountain- Stavislost.com
- Cobble Hill- Offonadventure.com- April 16th, 2015
- Black Mountain- Lakegeorge.com
- Erebus Mountain- Telemarkmike
- Sleeping Beauty- Protectadks.com- August 28th, 2020
- Buck Mountain- Protectadks.com- March 28th, 2021
- Five Mile Mountain- Protectadks.com- August 2nd, 2020
- Huckleberry Mountain- Andy Arthur- May 12th, 2012
- Thomas Mountain- Offonadventure.com- July 27th, 2013
- Brown Mountain- HikingViking
- Cat Mountain- Lakegeorge.com
- Fifth Peak- HikingViking
- French Point Mountain- Jean André Laverdure- October 18th, 2017
- First Peak- Ridgehiker
- Mt. Adams- Jessica Tabora- February 9th, 2015
- Mt. Arab- Protectadks.com- August 11th, 2020
- Azure Mountain- Lakeplaicdclublodges.com- August 26th, 2020
- Bald Mountain- adktaste.com
- Belfry Mountain- Stephanie Graudons- Outdoorproject.com
- Black Mountain Firetower- Anthony F. Hall- September 5th, 2023
- Blue Mountain- Trailforks.com- August 17th, 2020
- Buck Mountain Firetower- Gwendolyn Craig- November 5th, 2022
- Cathedral Rock- Stlctrails.com
- Goodnow Mountain- Experience Newcomb
- Gore Mountain- Protectadks.com- March 29th, 2021

- Hadley Mountain- Hadleymtfiretower.org
- Hurricane Mountain Firetower- Phil Brown- Adirondack Explorer- May 7th, 2010
- Kane Mountain- Douglas Fortman- October 15th, 2016
- Loon Lake Mountain- Protectadks.com- June 16th, 2020
- Lyon Mountain- Lawrence P. Gooley- May 14th, 2018
- Owls Head Mountain- Nick Catania- Outdoorproject.com
- Pillsbury Mountain- Nick Catania- Outdoorproject.com
- Poke-O-Moonshine Mountain- Mike Lynch- May 4th, 2023
- Snowy Mountain- Nick Catania- Outdoorproject.com
- Spruce Mountain- Recreation.gov
- Stillwater Mountain- Kurt Gardener- Kurtgardenerphotography.com
- St. Regis Mountain- Community News Reporters- Adirondackalmanack.com
- Swede Mountain- Warrencountyny.gov- August 13th, 2021
- Vanderwhacker Mountain- Protectadks.com- July 20th, 2020
- Wakely Mountain- Protectadks.com- June 6th, 2020
- Woodhull Mountain- Justin A. Levine- August 24th, 2019

(Mt.Marcy from Lake Tear of the Clouds)

My Adirondacks Journey
Log Book

(Summit of Cascade Mountain)

Printed in the USA
CPSIA information can be obtained
at www.ICGtesting.com
CBHW060613150824
13132CB00030B/287